PARES SCALES

For Individual Study
and Like-Instrument Class Instruction

by GABRIEL PARÈS

Revised and Edited by  histler

Published for:

- **Flute or Piccolo** . . . . .Parès-Whistler

  Clarinet . . . . .Parès-Whistler

  Oboe . . . . .Parès-Whistler

  Bassoon . . . . .Parès-Whistler

  Saxophone . . . . .Parès-Whistler

  Cornet, Trumpet or Baritone 𝄞 . . . . .Parès-Whistler

  French Horn, E♭ Alto or Mellophone . . . . . . .Parès-Whistler

  Trombone or Baritone 𝄢 . . . . .Parès-Whistler

  E♭ Bass . . . . .Parès-Whistler

  BB♭ Bass . . . . .Parès-Whistler

  Marimba, Xylophone or Vibes . . . . . . .Parès-Whistler-Jolliff

For Individual Study and Like-Instrument Class Instruction
(Not Playable by Bands or by Mixed-Instruments)

RUBANK®

HAL•LEONARD®
CORPORATION
7777 W. BLUEMOUND RD. P.O. BOX 13819 MILWAUKEE, WI 53213

Key of C Major
Long Tones to Strengthen Lips

Scale of C

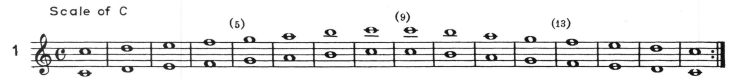

Also practice holding each tone for EIGHT counts.
When playing long tones, practice (1) ⊂ and (2) ⊂ ⊃

Embouchure Studies

Slur as many tones as possible

Slur as many tones as possible

4

Key of G Major
Long Tones to Strengthen Lips

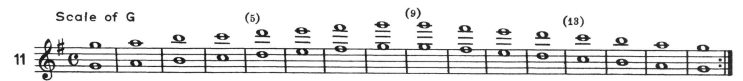

Also practice holding each tone for EIGHT counts.
When playing long tones, practice (1) $<$ and (2) $< >$.

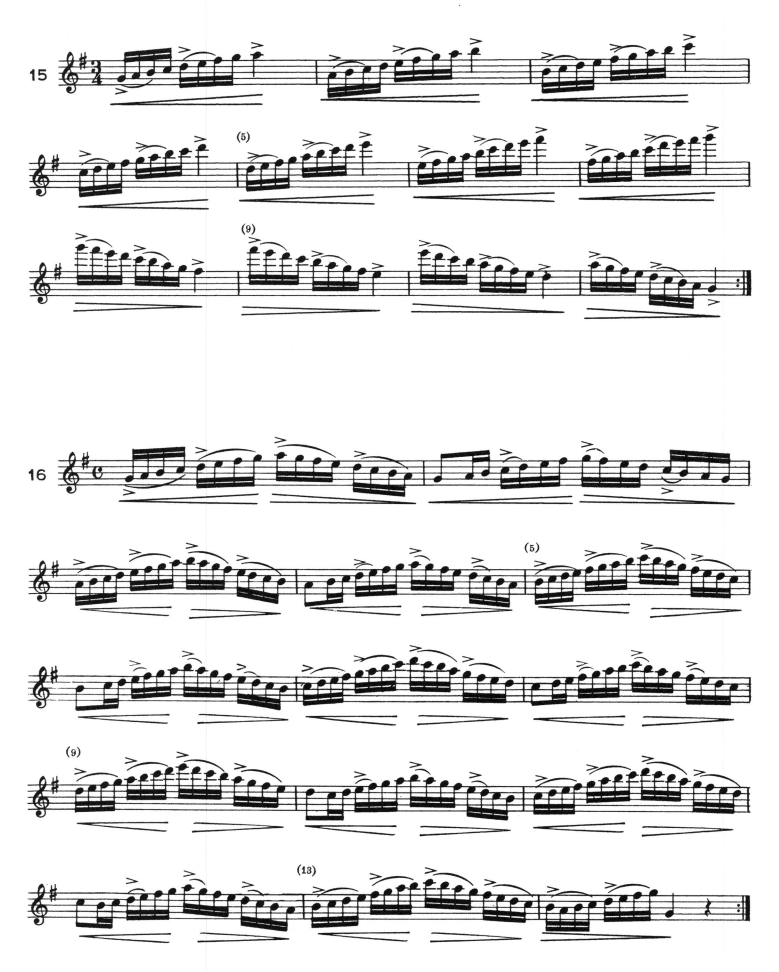

Embouchure Studies

Slur as many tones as possible

Key of F Major
Long Tones to Strengthen Lips

Scale of F

22

Also practice holding each tone for EIGHT counts.
When playing long tones, practice (1) $<$ and (2) $<>$.

23

24

25

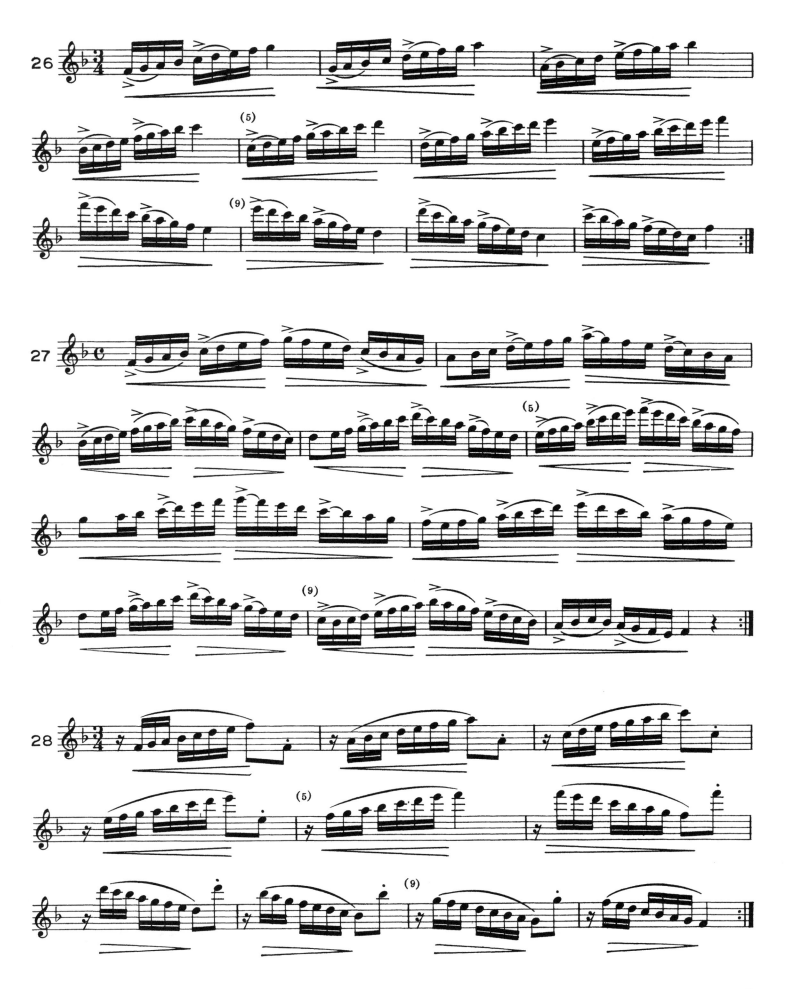

Embouchure Studies

Slur as many tones as possible

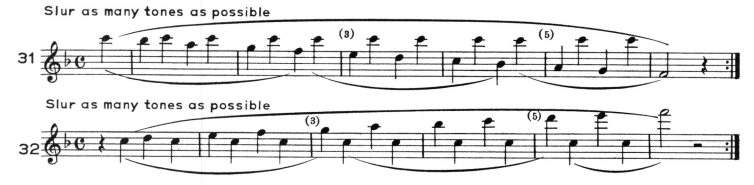

Key of D Major
Long Tones to Strengthen Lips

Scale of D

33

Also practice holding each tone for EIGHT counts.
When playing long tones, practice (1) $\longleftarrow$ and (2) $\longleftarrow\longrightarrow$.

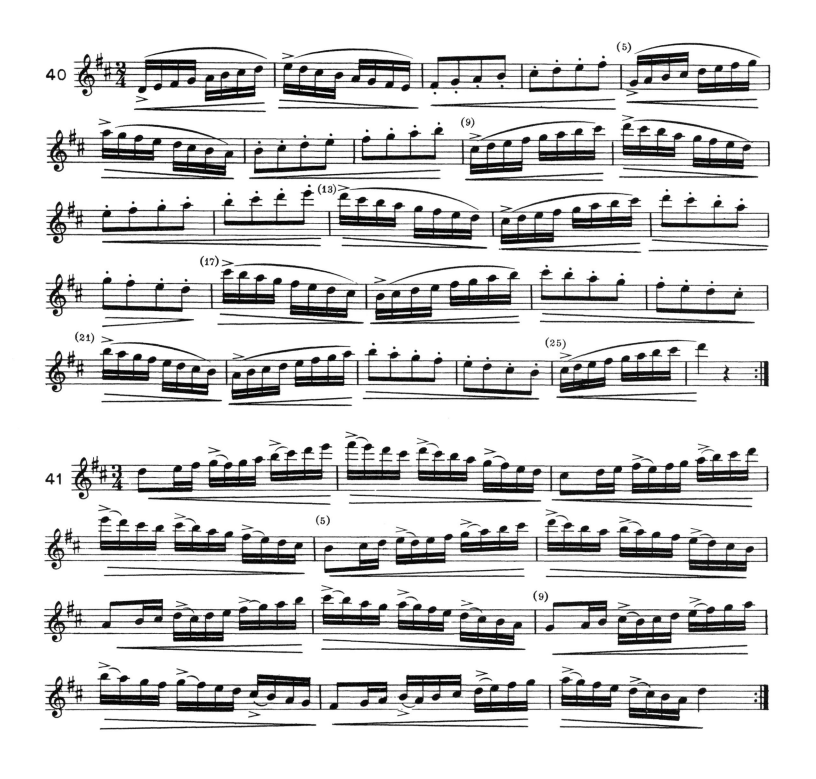

Embouchure Studies

Slur as many tones as possible

Slur as many tones as possible

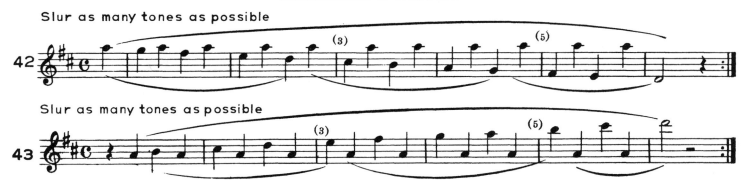

Key of Bb Major
Long Tones to Strengthen Lips

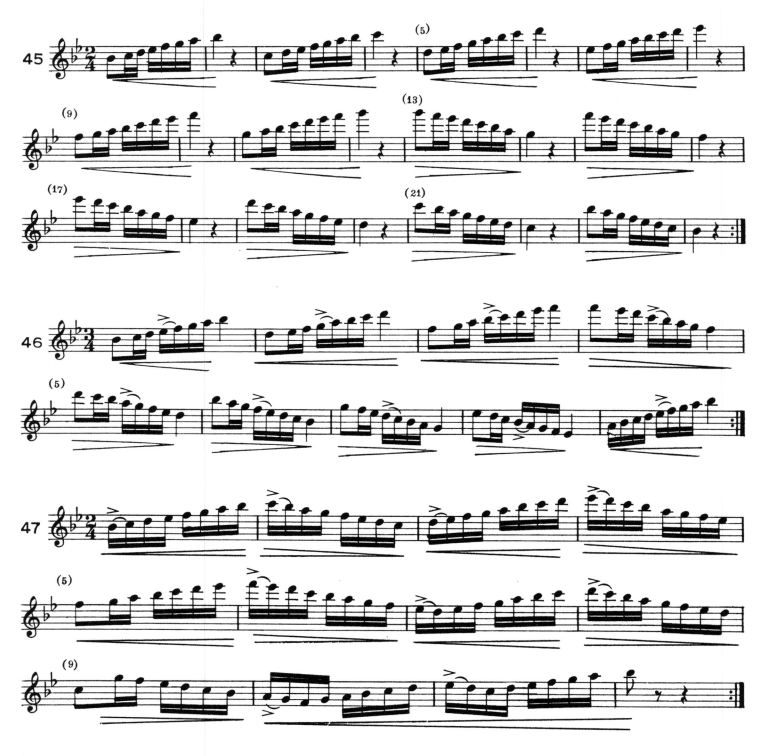

Also practice holding each tone for EIGHT counts.
When playing long tones, practice (1) ⟨ and (2) ⟨⟩.

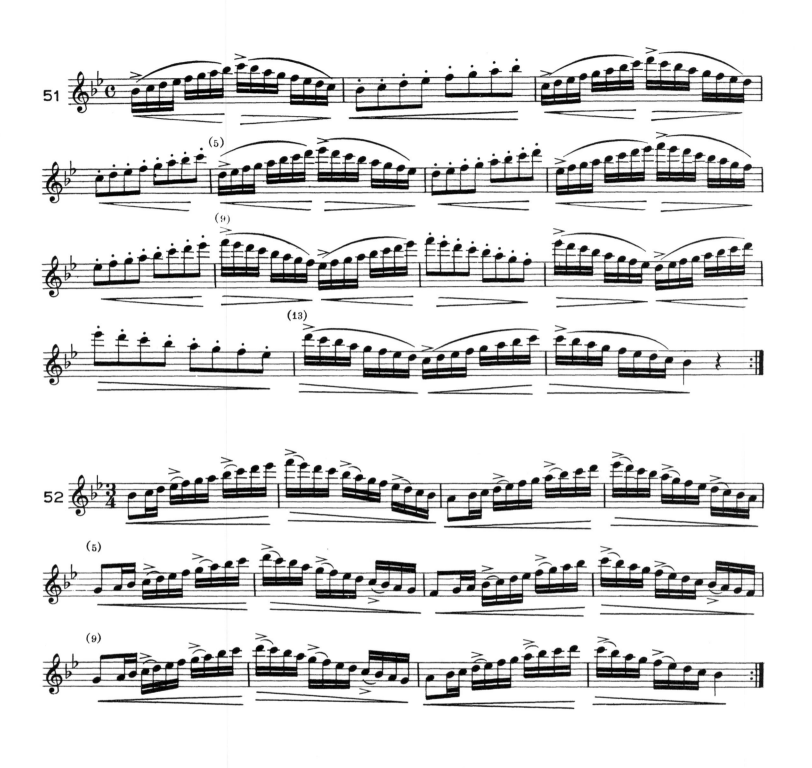

Embouchure Studies

Slur as many tones as possible

Slur as many tones as possible

Key of A Major
Long Tones to Strengthen Lips

Scale of A

55

Also practice holding each tone for EIGHT counts.
When playing long tones, practice (1) ⟨ and (2) ⟨ ⟩ .

56

57

58

Embouchure Studies

Slur as many tones as possible

Slur as many tones as possible

Key of Eb Major
Long Tones to Strengthen Lips

Scale of Eb

66

Also practice holding each tone for EIGHT counts.
When playing long tones, practice (1) < and (2) < >

67

68

69

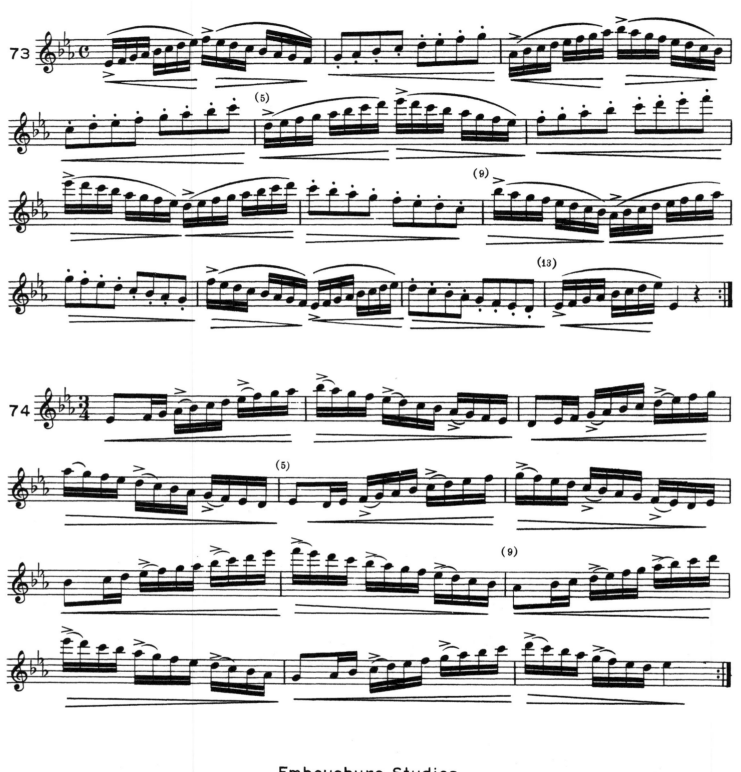

Embouchure Studies

Slur as many tones as possible

Slur as many tones as possible

Key of E Major
Long Tones to Strengthen Lips

Scale of E

Also practice holding each tone for EIGHT counts.
When playing long tones, practice (1) —◁ and (2) ◁▷ .

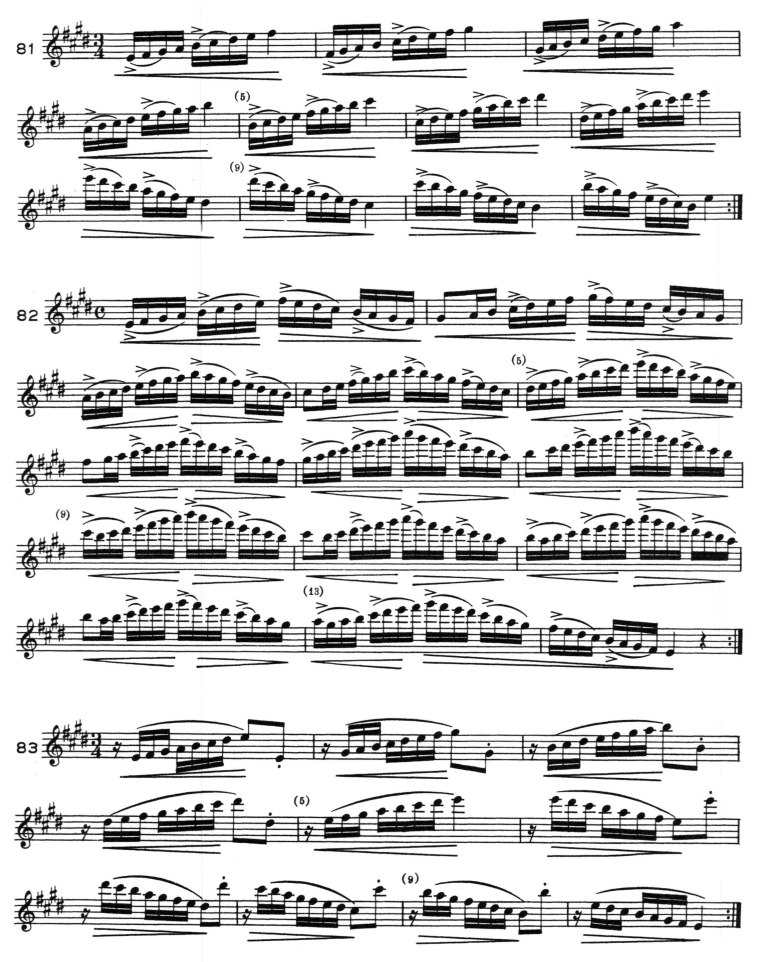

Embouchure Studies

Slur as many tones as possible

Slur as many tones as possible

Key of A♭ Major
Long Tones to Strengthen Lips

Also practice holding each tone for EIGHT counts.
When playing long tones, practice (1) ⟨ and (2) ⟨⟩

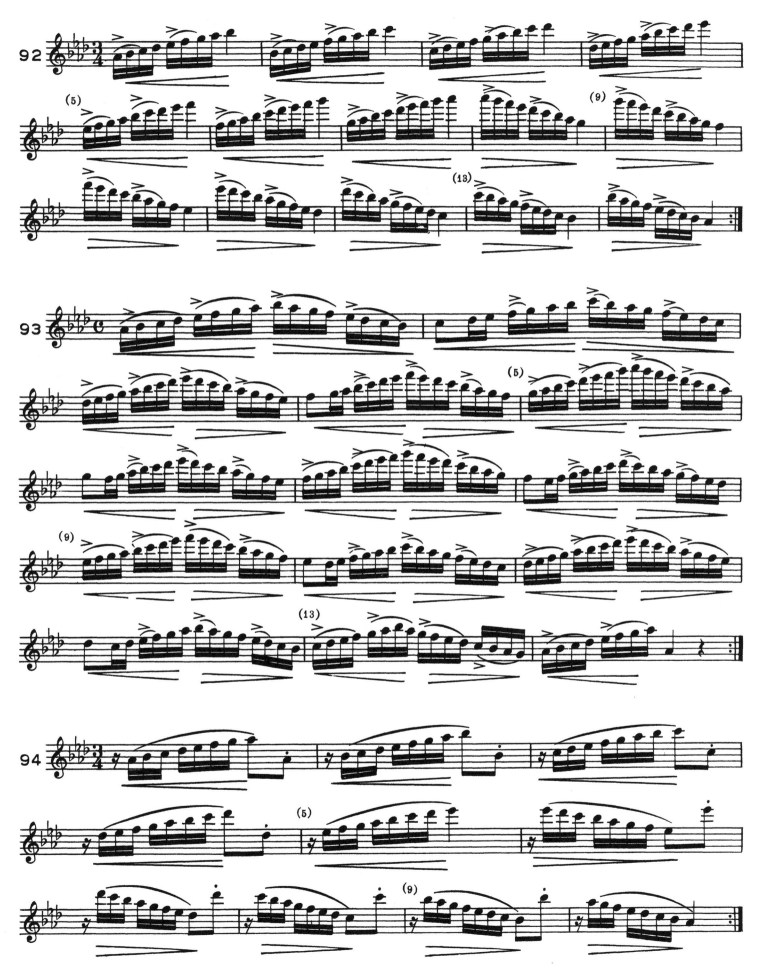

Embouchure Studies

Slur as many tones as possible

Slur as many tones as possible

Key of A Minor
(Relative to the Key of C Major)
Long Tones to Strengthen Lips

Scale of A Harmonic Minor

99

Scale of A Melodic Minor

100

Also practice holding each tone for EIGHT counts.
When playing long tones, practice (1) and (2)

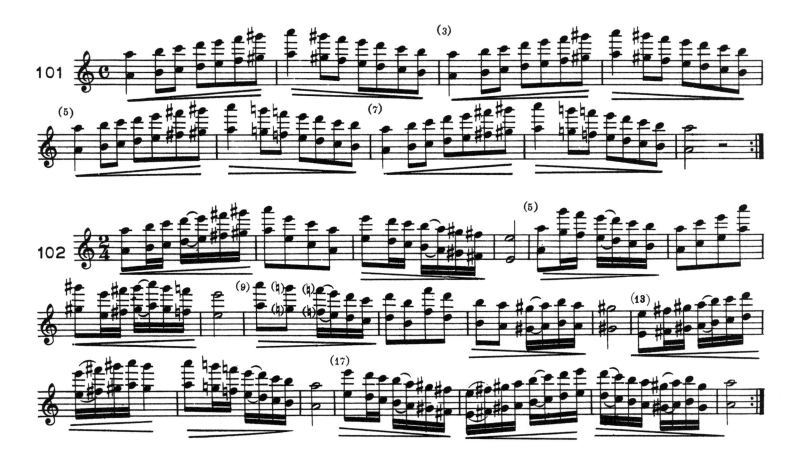

101

102

Embouchure Studies

Slur as many tones as possible

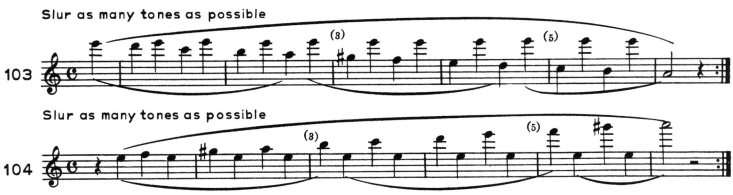

103

Slur as many tones as possible

104

Key of E Minor
(Relative to the Key of G Major)
Long Tones to Strengthen Lips

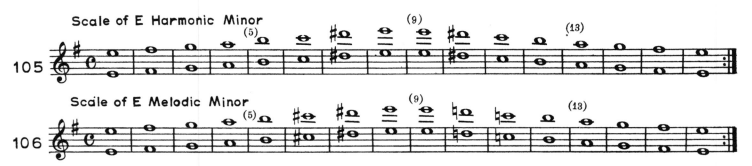

Scale of E Harmonic Minor

105

Scale of E Melodic Minor

106

Also practice holding each tone for EIGHT counts.
When playing long tones, practice (1) $<$ and (2) $<>$.

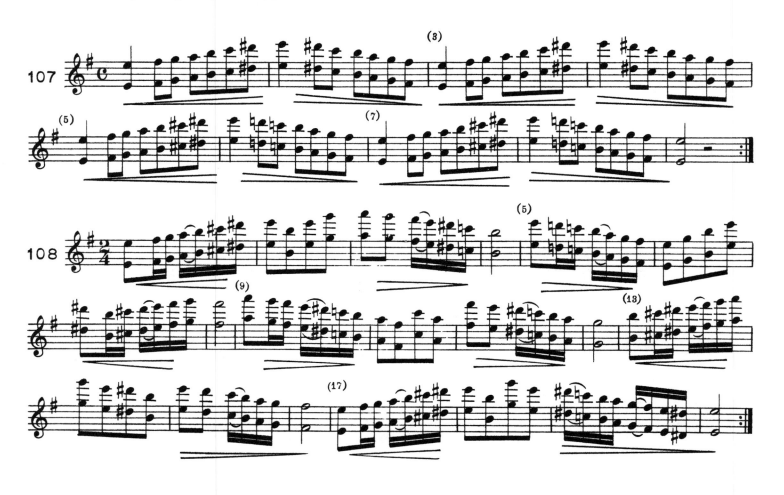

107

108

Embouchure Studies

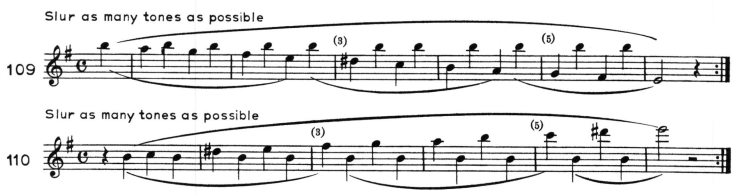

Slur as many tones as possible

109

Slur as many tones as possible

110

Key of D Minor
(Relative to the Key of F Major)
Long Tones to Strengthen Lips

Also practice holding each tone for EIGHT counts.

When playing long tones, practice (1) ⬡ and (2) ⬡.

Embouchure Studies

Slur as many tones as possible

Slur as many tones as possible

Key of B Minor
(Relative to the Key of D Major)
Long Tones to Strengthen Lips

Scale of B Harmonic Minor

Scale of B Melodic Minor

Also practice holding each tone for EIGHT counts.
When playing long tones, practice (1) < and (2) <> .

Embouchure Studies

Slur as many tones as possible

Slur as many tones as possible

Key of G Minor

(Relative to the Key of B♭ Major)
Long Tones to Strengthen Lips

Scale of G Harmonic Minor

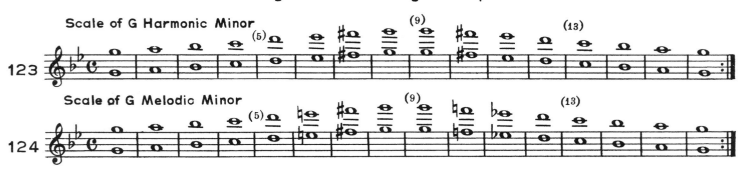

123

Scale of G Melodic Minor

124

Also practice holding each tone for EIGHT counts.
When playing long tones, practice (1) ⟨ and (2) ⟨ ⟩ .

125

126

Embouchure Studies

Slur as many tones as possible

127

Slur as many tones as possible

128

Key of F# Minor
(Relative to the Key of A Major)
Long Tones to Strengthen Lips

Scale of F# Harmonic Minor

129

Scale of F# Melodic Minor

130

Also practice holding each tone for EIGHT counts.
When playing long tones, practice (1) < and (2) < >.

131

132

Embouchure Studies

Slur as many tones as possible

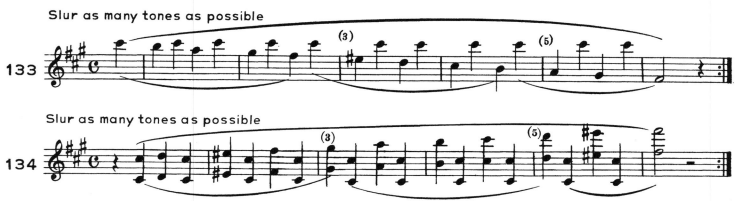

133

Slur as many tones as possible

134

Key of C Minor
(Relative to the Key of E♭ Major)
Long Tones to Strengthen Lips

Also practice holding each tone for EIGHT counts.
When playing long tones, practice (1) ⸺ and (2) ⸺ .

Embouchure Studies

Slur as many tones as possible

Slur as many tones as possible

Key of C# Minor
(Relative to the Key of E Major)
Long Tones to Strengthen Lips

Scale of C# Harmonic Minor

141

Scale of C# Melodic Minor

142

Also practice holding each tone for EIGHT counts.
When playing long tones, practice (1) ⟨ and (2) ⟨⟩

143

144

Embouchure Studies

Slur as many tones as possible

145

Slur as many tones as possible

146

Key of F Minor
(Relative to the Key of A♭ Major)
Long Tones to Strengthen Lips

Scale of F Harmonic Minor

147

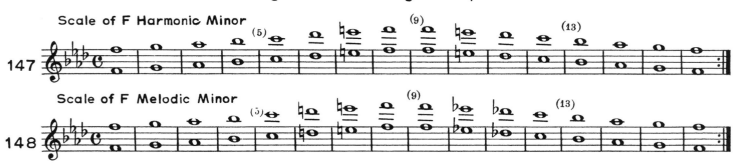

Scale of F Melodic Minor

148

Also practice holding each tone for EIGHT counts.
When playing long tones, practice (1) ⟨ and (2) ⟨⟩ .

149

150

Embouchure Studies

Slur as many tones as possible

151

Slur as many tones as possible

152

Major Scales

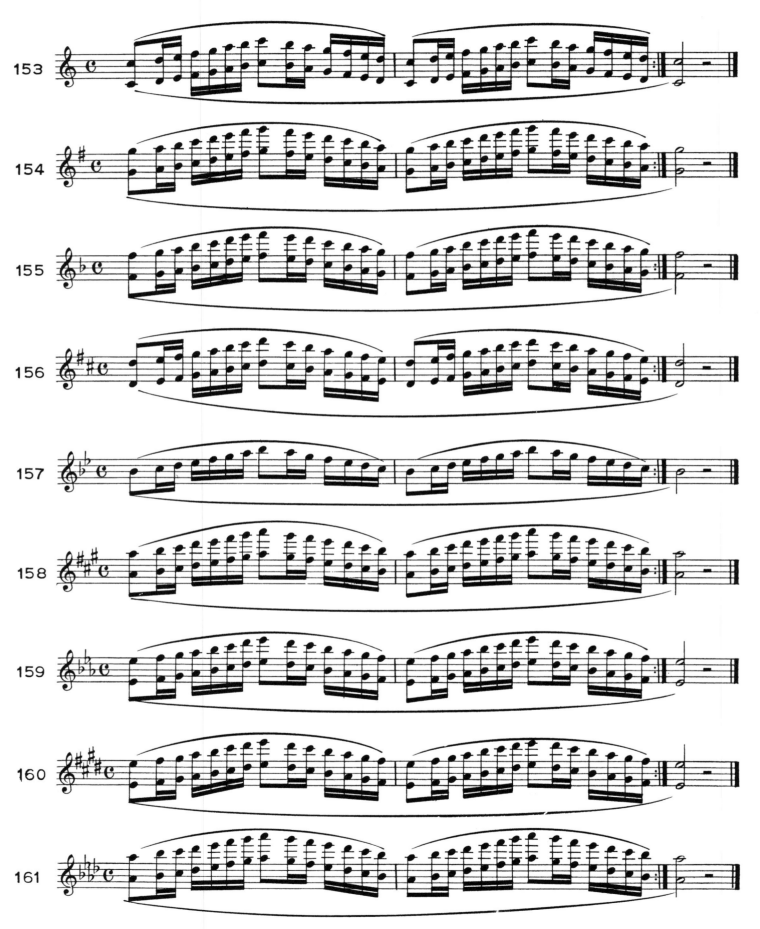

Harmonic Minor Scales

Melodic Minor Scales

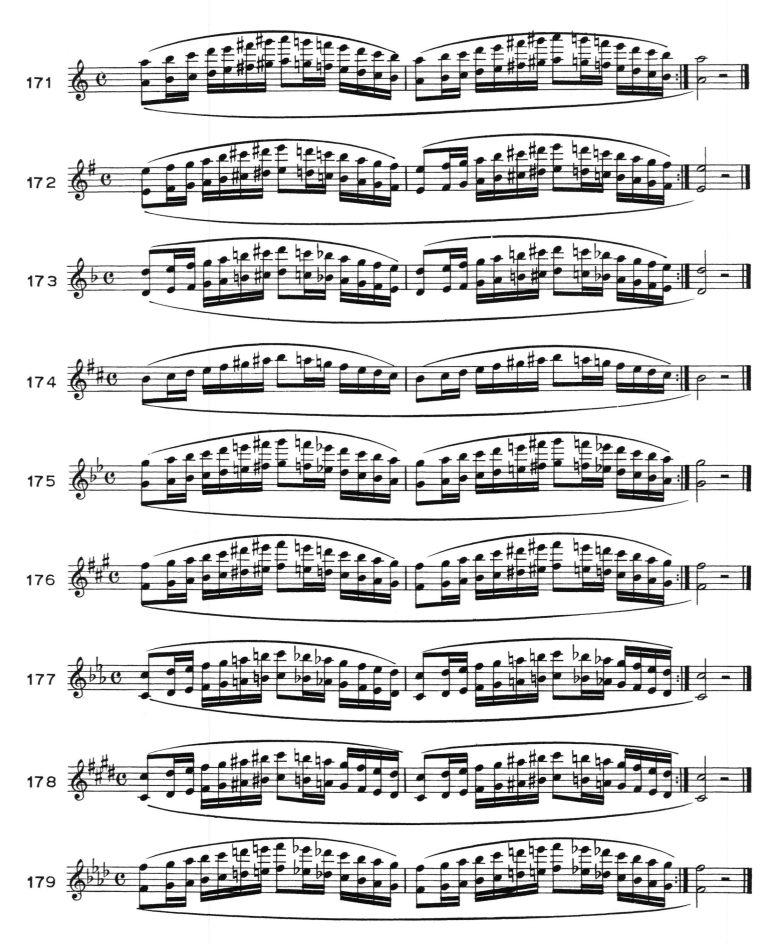

Arpeggios

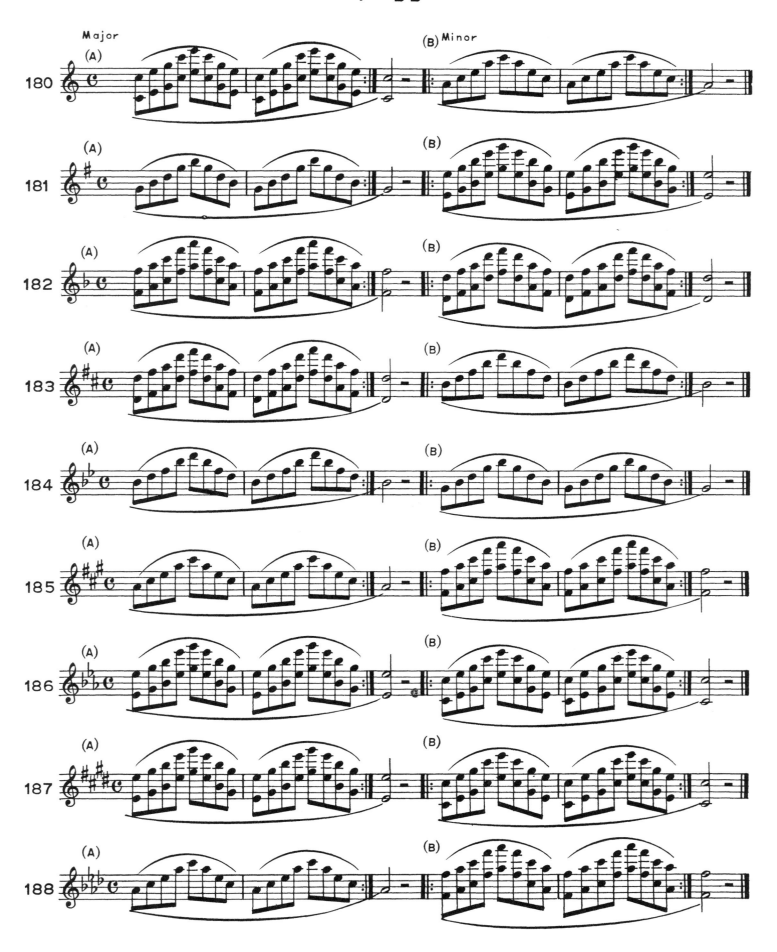

Chromatic Scales

Chromatic Scales in Triplets

Two Octave Chromatic Scales

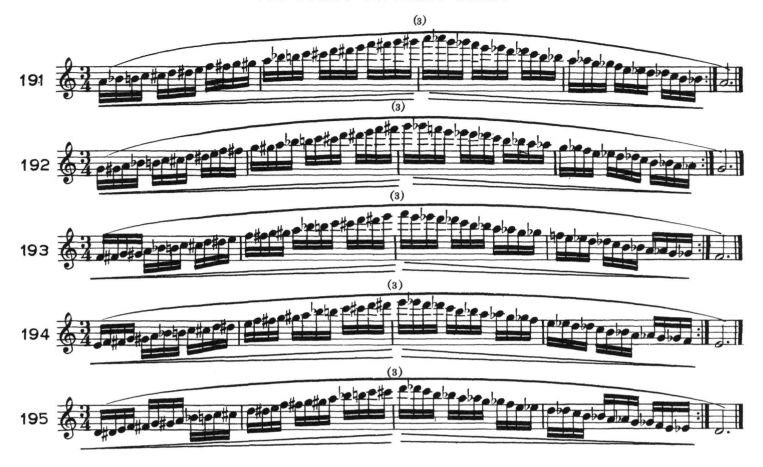

Two Octave Chromatic Scales in Triplets

Studies in Mechanism

Also practice each exercise an octave higher.

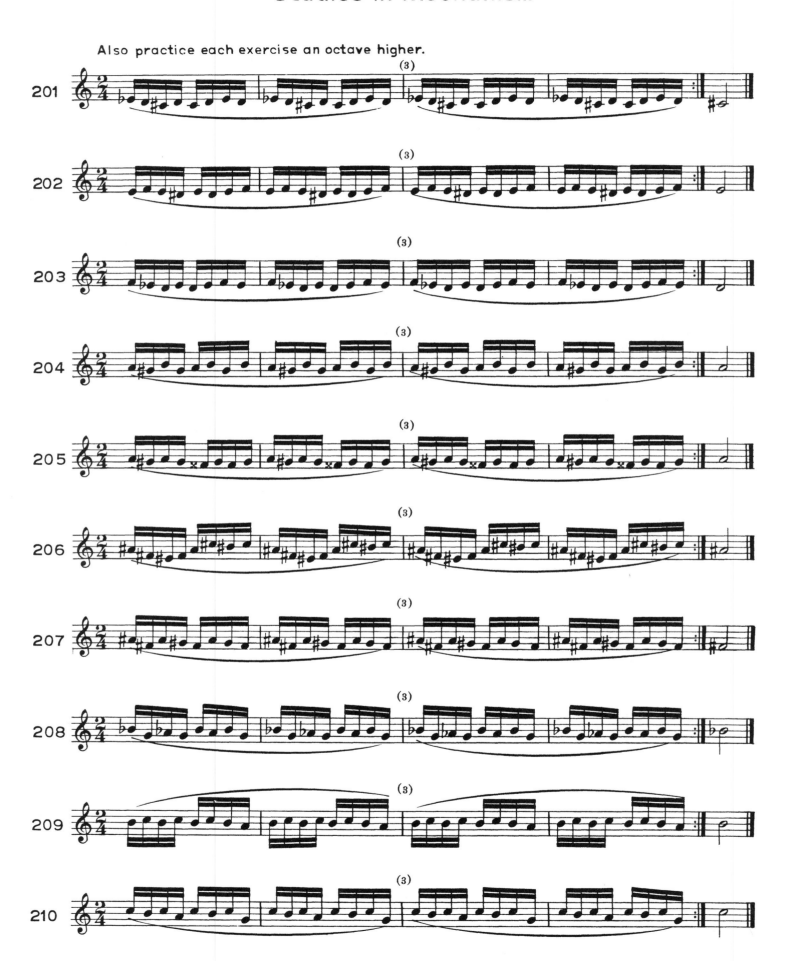

Scales in Thirds

Basic Exercises to Strengthen High Tones

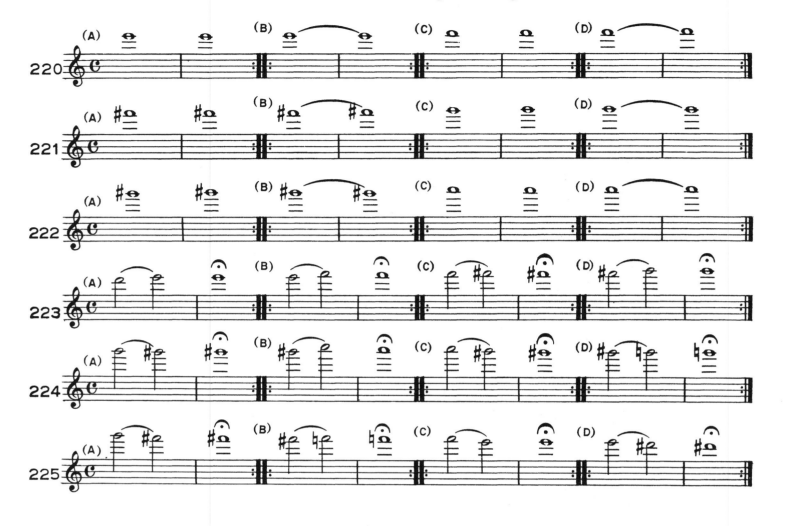

Short Studies in the High Register

(A) Also practice very slowly holding each tone for (1) FOUR counts, and (2) EIGHT counts.
   When playing long tones, practice (1) $<$ and (2) $<\!\!>$.
(B) Also practice very legato, (1) slurring each two tones, and (2) slurring each four tones.

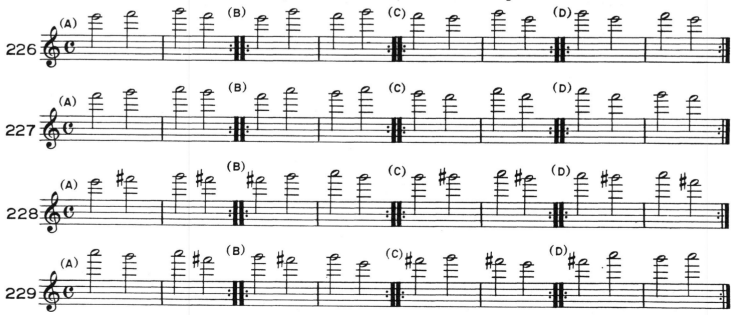

Intonation Studies

Also practice holding each tone for (1) FOUR counts, and (2) EIGHT counts.
Also practice (1) slurring each TWO tones, and (2) slurring each FOUR tones.
Listen carefully to the pitch at all times, and "humor" the tone when necessary.

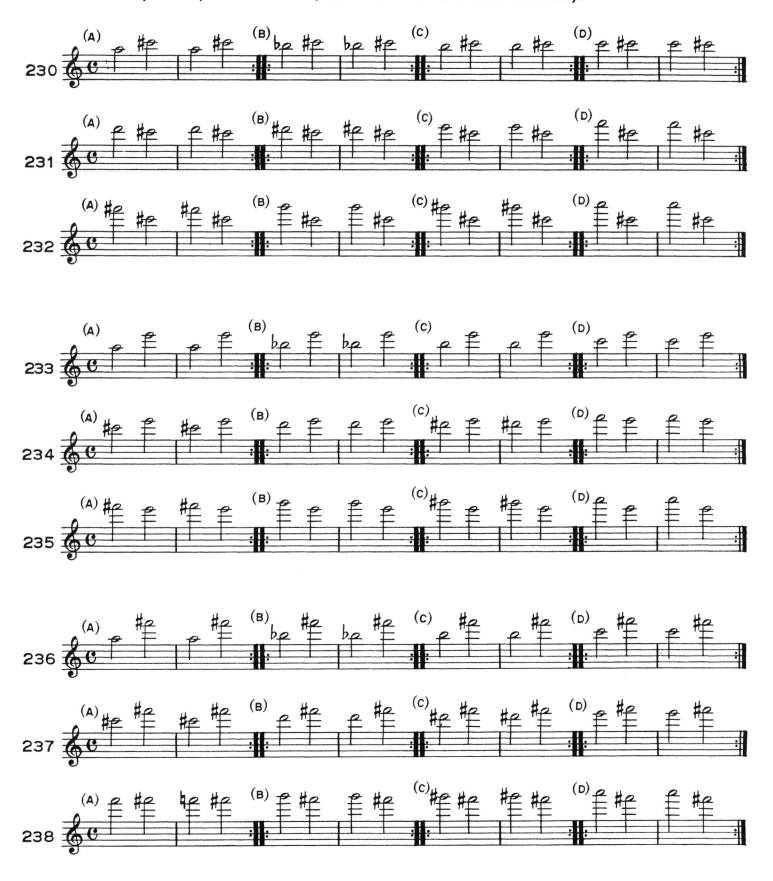

Velocity Studies

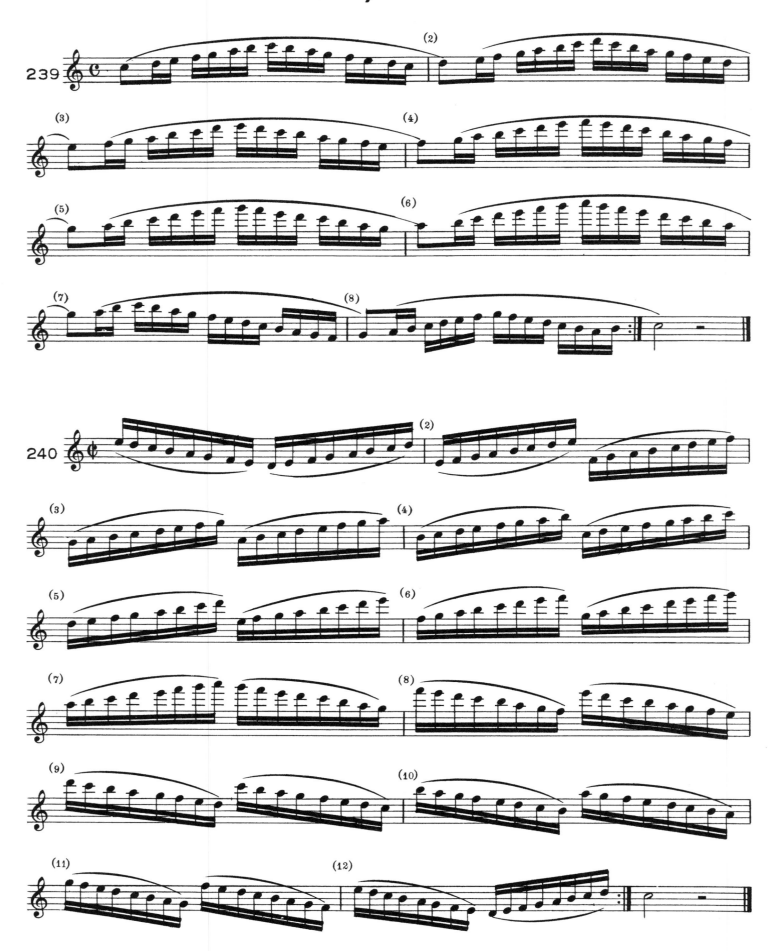